Watching the Seasons

By Edana Eckart

Welcome Books™

Children's Press®
A Division of Scholastic Inc.
New York / Toronto / London / Auckland / Sydney
Mexico City / New Delhi / Hong Kong
Danbury, Connecticut

Photo Credits: Cover © Matheisl/Getty Images; p. 5 © Walden Joura/Getty Images; p. 7 © Michael S. Yamashita/Corbis; p. 9 © Kelly-Mooney Photography/Corbis; p. 11 © Tom Till/Getty Images; p. 13 © Georgette Douwma/Getty Images; pp. 15, 19 © Getty Images; p. 17 © Photodisc

Contributing Editors: Shira Laskin and Jennifer Silate
Book Design: Michelle Innes

Library of Congress Cataloging-in-Publication Data

Eckart, Edana.
  Watching the seasons / by Edana Eckart.
    p. cm.—(Watching nature)
  Includes index.
  Summary: Simple text introduces facts about the four seasons.
  ISBN 0-516-27600-X (lib. bdg.)—ISBN 0-516-25937-7 (pbk.)
  1. Seasons—Juvenile literature. [1. Seasons] I. Title. II. Series.

QB637.4.E25 2004
508.2—dc21   2003010817

5374

Contents

1 Winter   4

2 Spring   8

3 Summer   12

4 Fall   16

5 New Words   22

6 To Find Out More   23

7 Index   24

8 About the Author   24

There are four **seasons** each year.

The first season of the year is **winter**.

4

The **weather** is very cold in the winter.

In some places it snows.

Spring starts after winter.

It gets warmer in the spring.

Flowers **bloom** and plants grow in the spring.

Summer comes after spring.

It gets hot in the summer.

In the summer, the Sun stays up in the sky later.

People play outside more.

Fall comes after summer.

The weather begins to get cooler.

The leaves on the trees change color in the fall.

The leaves turn yellow, orange, and red.

At the end of fall, winter starts again.

The four seasons are beautiful to watch.

New Words

bloom (**bloom**) when flowers open up

fall (**fawl**) the season between summer and winter

seasons (**see**-zuhnz) the times of year that have their own kinds of weather

spring (**spring**) the season between winter and summer

summer (**suhm**-uhr) the season that comes between spring and fall, when the weather is warmest

weather (**weth**-uhr) how hot or cold it is outside

winter (**wint**-uhr) the season between fall and spring, when the weather is coldest

22

To Find Out More

Books

*I Wonder Why the Sun Rises and Other Questions
About Time and Seasons*
by Brenda Walpole
Kingfisher Publications

The Reasons for Seasons
by Gail Gibbons
Holiday House, Inc.

Web Site

New Science: The First Day of Spring
http://kids.msfc.nasa.gov/News/2000/News-VernalEquinox.asp
Learn about the seasons and play games on this Web site.

Index

bloom, 10

fall, 16, 18, 20
flowers, 10

leaves, 18

plants, 10

seasons, 4, 20
snows, 6
spring, 8, 10,
    12

summer, 12,
    14, 16
Sun, 14

weather, 6, 16
winter, 4, 6, 8,
    20

About the Author
Edana Eckart has written several children's books. She enjoys bike riding with her family.

Reading Consultants
Kris Flynn, Coordinator, Small School District Literacy, The San Diego County Office of Education

Shelly Forys, Certified Reading Recovery Specialist, W.J. Zahnow Elementary School, Waterloo, IL

Paulette Mansell, Certified Reading Recovery Specialist, and Early Literacy Consultant, TX